A book for precocious grown-ups, about a little man
who lives at The White House HOTEL

Mean
MR. TRUMP

Written by Ian Mather
Illustrated by Lindsey Cirmotich

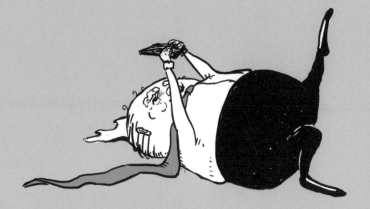

I am Mr Trump
I am seventy
something?

It's been a few years since I was elected
Supreme Leader of America
A year is like a whole TWELVE MONTHS!

It feels like it's been so long
and I think it's about time I let you inside
to show you what my life is really like

I live in The White House
Do you know what that is?
It's okay I didn't until a few years ago

It's like a big fancy hotel for important men from America

And EVEN some from KENYA!

A lot sure has happened
Since I was elected God King of America
and I've had to say goodbye
to a lot of good friends

Luckily nobody ever really leaves

And when you live at The White House
EVERYONE wants to be your friend
I've made TONS of new ones

I live in the penthouse apartment
It's all the way on the twentieth floor

This is my elevator man
His name is Mr Clancy
He's super silly
Every night he tells the same joke
I get on and say "take me to the twentieth floor Mr Clancy"
And he always looks at me over his sunglasses and says the same thing
"Sir there are only six floors in the building"
He's so funny
That joke always tickles me DEEP in my tummy
and I collapse in a fit of laughter
"A hotel with only six floors?" I say "That doesn't even make sense"
And Mr Clancy always sighs and says
"Again Mr President this isn't a hotel this is The White House"
He thinks I don't know what he's doing
but I know EXACTLY what he's doing
So I smile my cunning little smile and say
"not a hotel huh
then why is there an elevator attendant?"
Then he frowns and says sternly "I'm not an elevator attendant
I'm with the Secret Service
Now are you ready to go to bed?
It's past ten o'clock"

Mr Clancy is no fun

Sometimes when Mr Clancy IS feeling fun
he lets me play hide and seek
He says I need to get really good at hiding
I don't know why
I just do what I'm told!

Sometimes I hide in the Oval Office
This is extra tricky though
because some IDIOT didn't put any corners in there
So the only place to hide
is behind the bust of Frederick Douglass

The very best hiding spot though
is in the White House Library
It's huge and has tons of books

Books are like little TVs
but they don't have any pictures
They only have words
Every time I look at one I get SO bored

I hate books
They're useless
Except for hats
They make great hats

Nobody ever looks for me in the library

Can you believe I have my own room all to myself?
Nobody EVER sleeps in it with me
Isn't that great?

Everything in it is gold
EVEN THE MATTRESS!
Can you believe that!?
There's also a big chandelier on the ceiling that has over five-thousand diamonds

Sometimes I like to hang from it and pretend I'm a monkey!

This is my Turtle
His name is Mitch

When you're the ruler of America
you can have any pet you want
As long as you keep them on a leash

Mitch loves to eat leaves
right out of my hand!

This is my Hobby Horse
His name is Mike

Most days I just lay around
and brush his hair
but sometimes

I ride him down the hall
like a REAL PONY!

One of the great things about being president
is you never have to clean

I have a maid who cleans everything up for me
Her name is Kelly
She's a GENIUS!
She makes everything look spotless without cleaning anything at all

She says her cleaning style is very alternative
I don't know what that means
but whenever we have guests over
they never actually see the mess I make
because Kelly is always pointing at something
completely unrelated to it!

Don't tell her this
But I think I have a crush on Kelly
She has white teeth
and her hair reminds me of fresh hay
I always make sure to have plenty of mints
whenever she's around

The hard part about being president
is that you have to work ALL DAY
and you have to be good at so many things

Luckily I got elected because I'm good at most everything

Like shaking hands

And signing my name

And playing golf

And cleaning coal

And building walls

And putting OTHER kids in time-out

And dressing up like a wizard
I think I make a really GRAND wizard!

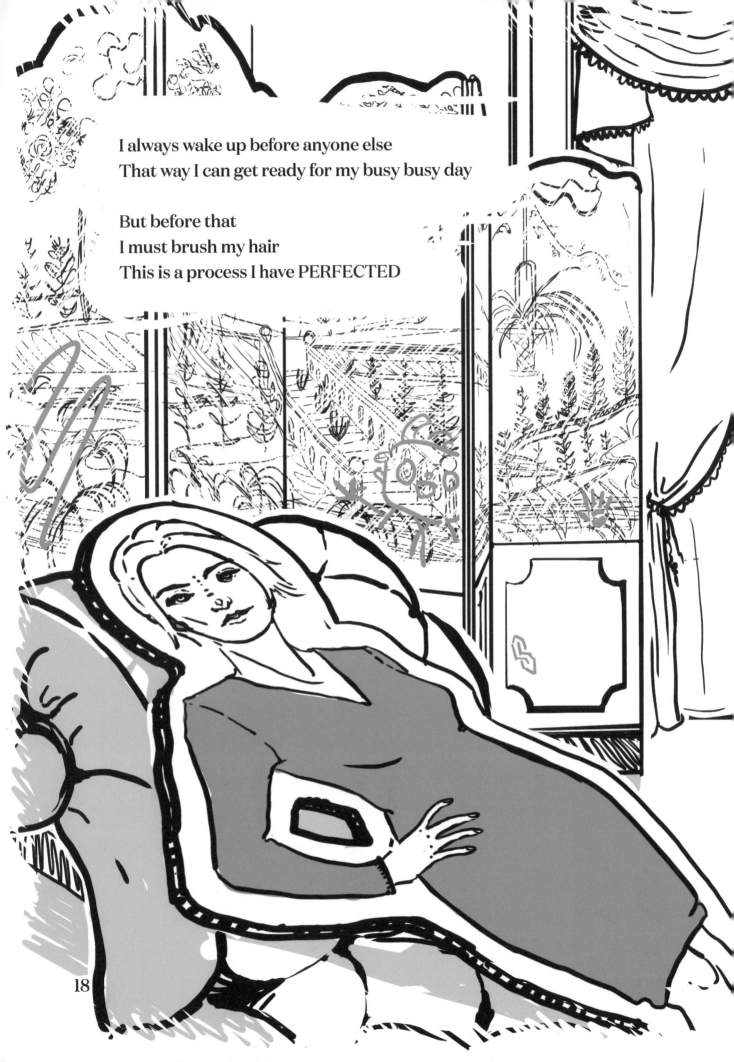

I always wake up before anyone else
That way I can get ready for my busy busy day

But before that
I must brush my hair
This is a process I have PERFECTED

18

I go into my dressing room
get out my little step-stool so I can see the mirror
and pick up my ivory brush that my smart son gave me

It's made out of a real dead elephant!

First I take my comb and brush front to back
then side to side

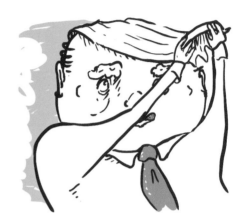

THEN back to front

Then up and down
and left to right

THEN

up down swipe it to the left across the back along the neck toss it up then mash it down spit on your hand shake it out tease the bangs ducktail the back comb it to the side massage the scalp fluff it up touch your toes do a little shimmy dip it in the toilet dance on your right foot dance on your left foot swirl the comb say a prayer and then

Let it fall

After I'm ready
I go say hi to my old friend Steve

Steve doesn't technically have a job anymore
but he still lives here at the hotel
He says he's here to "haunt the White House"
but I think he just needs a place to stay

People do get awful scared
when they see Steve around
and I don't blame them

Steve's probably the scariest person I know!

Sometimes he waits in my room dressed as a ghost with a pointy hat
and that always scares the pants right off me

So every morning
to get revenge I sneak into Steve's room
hiding as he gets out of the shower
and when he least expects it
I POP OUT
and try and scare him so he drops his towel
But it never works

Nothing scares Steve
except for something he calls the caucasian extinction scenario
but I don't know what that is
So I just growl at him like a bear

Then I visit my OTHER friend Steve

We always brush our teeth together every morning
He says it's important to keep our teeth nice and white

Nice and white

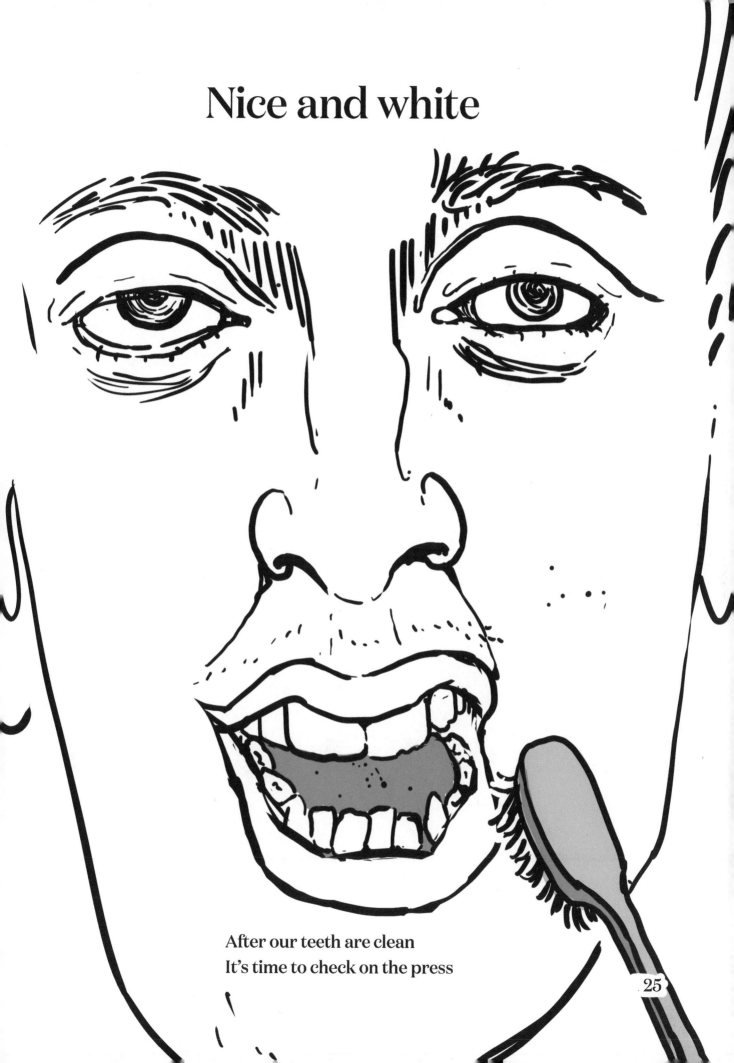

After our teeth are clean
It's time to check on the press

I like to keep the press in the basement
where they can be nice and comfy

We used to have a funny clown down there
but I don't know where he went
SAD!
So now this smokey eyed witch
tells them fables to pass the time

Sometimes they can get real antsy
especially when they're hungry
but don't worry
I feed them five to ten tweets a day
and that usually keeps them satisfied

The thing I hate most of all is when Mr Schumer comes in my office
He's always trying to tell me what to do
and I HATE when people tell me what to do
But I know how to make him nice and angry

He comes in and says "Mr President we have to compromise"
and I say in a funny voice "Mr President we have to compromise"
And then he says "You can't just appoint ANYONE to the Supreme Court"
And I say "You can't just appoint ANYONE to the Supreme Court"
And he says "stop it"
And I say "stop it" right back at him
And then he looks at me with angry eyes
and I look right back at him with my angry eyes
and then he pouts his lips
and I pout my lips right back at him
And he says "that's enough Mr President"
And I say "that's enough Mr President"
And then he stands and says "alright then I'll just leave"
And then I stand too and say "alright then I'll just leave"
And then he walks towards the door
and I walk toward the door too
and then he shouts "Kelly come talk to him please!"
And then I shout "Kelly come talk to him please!"
Then Kelly rushes in to calm him down but Mr Schumer is almost in tears by now
And he says "Kelly he won't stop copying me"
And I say "Kelly he won't stop copying me"
And he screams "STOP COPYING ME!"
And I scream "STOP COPYING ME!"
Then Kelly puts her arm around his shoulders
and says "we'll just push the meeting until after his nap"
and she ushers him out

I'm always glad to see Mr Schumer leave

If I'm being honest with you
Being Overlord of America got PRETTY boring after a while
Mostly I just sign papers all day
I know it sounds easy
but after about three my little wrist starts to cramp up
That's okay though
Mitch usually helps me finish the rest

And finally after all the day's work
I get to hang with my good friend Vladimir

He can be really fun most of the time
but he is a little different
He plays weird games that I've never heard of before
like Phone Tap Extravaganza
and Browser History Scavenger Hunt

He also likes to do this thing
where we go around the whole house
and put cameras in all the rooms
EVEN the bathrooms

Vlad can be so strange sometimes
but I like him cause his name sounds like a vampire

AND he likes to ride horses too
And that's what Mike is here for

Sometimes I miss my new friend Kimmy

I only met him once
but we became best friends INSTANTLY!
He's sure knows how to have fun!

We spent all day playing with his nukes

And pranking his relatives

And shaking hands!
Kimmy gives the best handshakes
We shook hands almost ALL NIGHT!

Maybe one day Kimmy can live here
In the hotel with ME!
That would be such a dream

We could shake hands EVERY DAY!

My absolute favorite part of the day
is TV time
I LOVE watching TV
and I make sure and savor it whenever I get the chance
because I'm only allowed to watch for ten hours a day
CAN YOU BELIEVE IT!?

Some of my best friends are on TV
Which is great because every show is about me
And sometimes they even let me CALL IN!

Whenever TV time starts
I do a celebratory cartwheel

Kelly and I watch together
and every time I see myself
I turn to her and say
"look Kelly those are my friends!"
and then she pats me on the head
and says "I know I know
but let's change the channel just for a minute"

That's when I notice that other people in the TV can be big bullies
who say mean mean things
And then I start to cry
and wail
and throw a HUGE tantrum

And in between my sobs
I say "KELLY
YOU HAVE TO
TELL THEM
THEY'RE WRONG!"
and she says "I will tomorrow"
Then she scolds me
and spanks me with a Forbes
and tells me to go in the other room until I calm down
and that I shouldn't be acting this way

But after all I am only seventy
something?

When you're the president
people forget that you have feelings too

When I get down
I like to spend time in this room where I can finally be alone

It's my favorite place in the whole house
It has everything that I like

It has walls that are covered in mirrors

My favorite coin

a brass tweeting throne
for when I'm EXTRA upset

and even a golden shower!

After I'm nice and calm
Kelly lets me know that it's time to go to bed
Then she takes me to my room
sets out my jammies
and tucks me in

I try to fall asleep right away
but it doesn't usually happen
At night everything seems so enormously dark
And I see the things that scare me the most
A big ghostly monster that looks like my dad picks me up
and drops me into a dark endless well

And I'm surrounded by werewolves goblins and ghouls
and they're all yelling at me
telling me that I'm not good enough
WAS never good enough
WILL NEVER BE good enough
They say I'm a disappointment
They say the people hate me
They say my friends hate me
They say EVEN I hate me!

I try to run away but the well is so endlessly deep
and I'm running out of air
but I keep climbing
and clawing
until I'm finally back in my bed
Safe

That's when I call in all of my friends
Kelly
Steve
The other Steve
Mr Clancy
Mike the horse
Mitch the turtle
Sarah the witch
Vladamir
and yes
even Mr Schumer
And we all crawl into my bed
and cuddle until we fall asleep

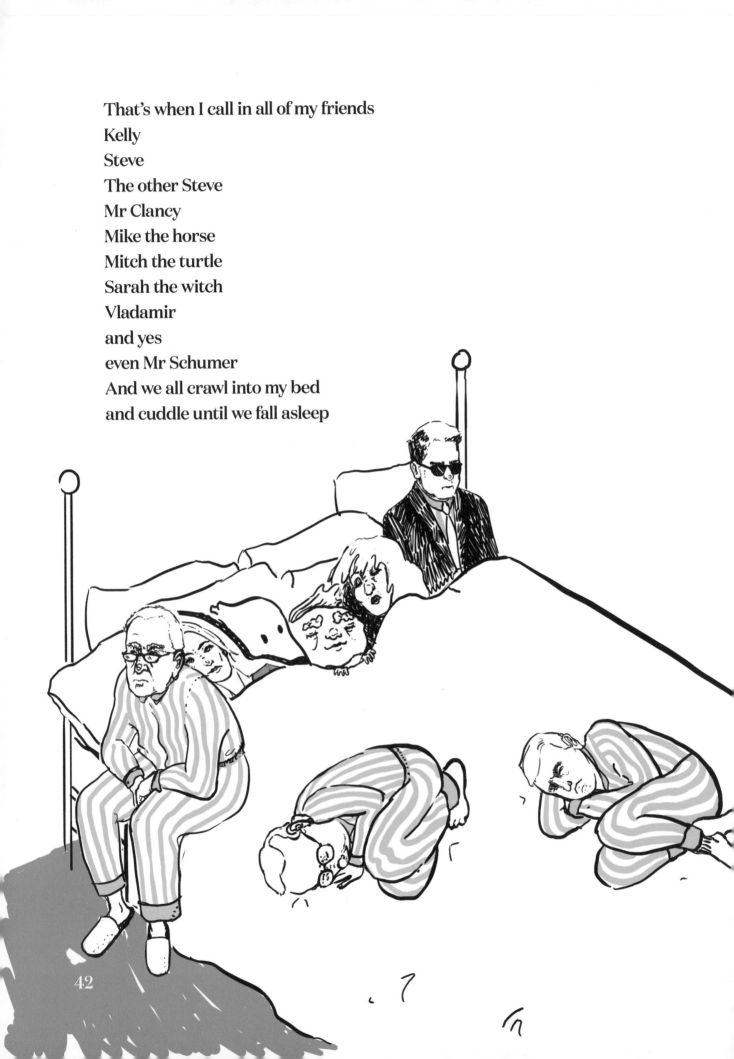

And right before I drift into my sweet sweet dreams
I look out of the door
and think
Oh my
there's so much to do
Tomorrow I think I'll pretend to be a king

Ooooooooh I absolutely love The White House Hotel

@MEANMRTRUMP
@IANXMATHER
@LINDSEYCIRMOTICH
WWW.MEANMRTRUMP.COM

CPSIA information can be obtained
at www.ICGtesting.com
Printed in the USA
BVHW02n0823251018
530843BV00010B/34/P